INTRODUCTION

1 Radioisotopes which emit gamma radiation and high-energy electron beam generators have been used in industry, medicine and research for many years in the UK and throughout the world. Their main application has been in medical product sterilisation, various food treatments, plastics curing and polymerisation, semi-conductor manufacture and gemstone irradiation to bring about colour changes. The radiation safety of these applications is the subject of this guidance.

Radiation hazards

2 Gamma radiation and electron beams interact with materials by causing ionisation in the atoms of which they are composed. This process is harmful to cells in living tissue and may either kill them directly or cause them to mutate (change genetically) in a way that may increase the exposed person's risk of developing cancer later in life. In the case of exposure to very large gamma sources and high-energy electron beam devices, such as those used for sterilisation, cell damage can be so severe that acute effects such as skin burns and radiation sickness occur soon after exposure; this can cause death which, depending on the exposure severity, may occur within a few weeks or even hours of exposure.

3 It is therefore vitally important that irradiators are designed and constructed so that personal exposure does not take place. However, although personal exposure to irradiator sources and generators is harmful, it is nonetheless precisely this ability to kill cells that makes their radiation so effective for large-scale sterilisation, particularly of medical products and foodstuffs.

Restriction of exposure

4 The law requires personal access to irradiator sources and generators to be restricted so far as is reasonably practicable (Ionising Radiations Regulations 1985[1] (IRR85), regulation 6), especially during plant commissioning, operation, adjustment, maintenance, repair and servicing. This control is usually achieved by the use of engineered features such as shielding and by the use of design features such as safety interlocks which prevent human access to irradiation chambers when dangerous radiation levels exist.

5 Experience has shown that gamma and electron beam irradiation facilities can be designed to have shielding sufficient to restrict radiation exposures, of those who work at the facility, to no more than that received by the general public from environmental radiation.

6 Radioactive source irradiator enclosures are categorised as follows:

Category I	self-contained, dry source storage irradiator;
Category II	panoramic, dry source storage irradiator;
Category III	self-contained, wet source storage irradiator;
Category IV	panoramic, wet source storage irradiator.

Examples of these categories are shown in Figures 1 to 4.

7 Category I and III installations are mainly found in research applications; they tend to be designed to deliver high doses to small items. Industrial applications such as large-scale sterilisation facilities are usually Category II or IV installations.

8 Category I units are generally housed in a laboratory or other designated room to which only authorised workers have access. Worker access restriction also applies to Category III devices but these tend to be installed in a room or building which has been specifically designed for the purpose.

Irradiator sources

9 The most common radionuclide is Cobalt-60. It has a long half-life (5.27 years) so that source change frequency is minimised; it emits two high-energy gamma photons (1.17 and 1.33MeV) which are highly penetrating. Cobalt in solid form is also insoluble and non-friable. It has a high melting point (1492°C) which reduces the risk of contamination if source containment fails, for example during a fire.

10 Caesium-137 has also been used in some installations around the world but has become less popular in recent years because its solubility makes it more difficult to contain for long periods. It also emits a single, lower energy photon (0.66 MeV) which means that much larger amounts of radioactivity are needed to produce a dose rate equivalent to that of Cobalt-60.

LEGAL REQUIREMENTS

Health and Safety at Work etc Act 1974[5]

11 The Health and Safety at Work etc Act 1974 (HSW) is the 'enabling act' under which a number of statutory instruments are made. This section summarises those which are particularly relevant to work with ionising radiation.

12 The HSW Act itself places a number of general duties on employers and employees. Sections 2 and 3 place duties on employers to assure the health and safety of their employees and others, so far as is reasonably practicable.

13 Section 6 places a duty on designers, manufacturers, importers, suppliers, erectors and installers to ensure that, so far as is reasonably practicable, an article used at work is so designed and constructed that it will be safe and without risk to health when it is being set up, used, cleaned or maintained. For articles used in work with ionising radiation, this duty is extended by IRR85, regulation 32(1) to include restriction of exposure of employees and other persons. Information must also be provided about safe article and substance use in workplaces. These duties have particular relevance to irradiation plants because exposure risks associated with the sources or generators they use are significant and can only be effectively controlled by good design, fabrication and competent operation.

The Ionising Radiations Regulations 1985 (IRR85)[1]

14 These Regulations, which were made under the HSW Act, set out legal requirements for all work with ionising radiation sources and generators. The Regulations are supported by an Approved Code of Practice (ACOP)[2] which gives practical guidance on appropriate ways to meet them. For irradiation facilities, enforcement of the Regulations falls exclusively to the Health and Safety Executive (HSE). Most of the guidance given in this document is about how to comply with this statutory instrument.

The Food (Control of Irradiation) Regulations 1990[6]

15 These Regulations specify the requirements for the irradiation of foodstuffs. In England and Wales they are administered jointly by the Ministry of Agriculture, Fisheries and Food, the Department of Health and the Welsh Office. In Scotland, responsibility rests with the Secretary of State for Scotland. Food irradiation is a licensed activity and cannot take place until the employer has obtained the necessary approval from the licensing authority. Food irradiation licences are additional to any other approvals needed to operate irradiation plants.

The Radioactive Substances Act 1993 (RSA93)[7]

Registration

16 The Act regulates the keeping of radioactive materials and the disposal of radioactive wastes; its purpose is to restrict radiation exposure arising from radioactive

substances entering the environment. The Act makes provision for registration of users of radioactive materials and provides for authorisation by the Secretary of State for the accumulation and disposal of radioactive waste.

17 Every employer who keeps or uses significant amounts of radioactive substances in the form of sealed sources is required by section 7 of the Act to be in possession of a Certificate of Registration issued by the Environment Agency or, if his company is in Scotland, the Scottish Environmental Protection Agency. Certain exemptions apply to irradiation facilities on licensed nuclear sites.

Authorisation for disposal

18 At the end of their useful life, sources used in irradiators will still be highly radioactive and must only be disposed of through a properly authorised organisation. This is normally arranged by radioactive source suppliers.

19 In the event of source tube leakage in a Category III or IV facility, significant amounts of radioactive ion-exchange resins may arise. Authorisation for the accumulation, short-term storage and eventual disposal of this material must be obtained from the appropriate agency.

Transport of radioactive materials

20 As elsewhere in the world, transport is highly regulated in the UK because of the often significant risks associated with moving radioactive materials. In the UK, the Department of the Environment, Transport and the Regions (DETR) has responsibility for radioactive materials transport regulation. Employers who need advice about the regulatory requirements which apply to their work or about the relevant enforcement agency should contact the Radioactive Materials Transport Division within DETR. UK regulations are similar in scope and requirement to model regulations developed by the International Atomic Energy Agency (IAEA) in the 1996 edition of document IAEA ST-1.[8]

21 The movement of radioactive sources by road is subject to the Radioactive Material (Road Transport) (Great Britain) Regulations 1996 (SI 1996 No 1350)[9] made under the Radioactive Material (Road Transport) Act 1991. These Regulations apply not only to public highways but to any road to which there is public access. The DETR exercises control by requiring those involved in the transport of radioactive sources (eg consignors, carriers etc) to set up appropriate quality assurance programmes which address all aspects of transport operations. These programmes are regularly audited. Enforcement is by DETR inspectors or traffic examiners.

22 In general, transport regulations set out packaging, labelling and documentation requirements for radioactive material consignment. These duties are mainly the consignor's; however consignees, carriers and drivers also need to be aware of regulatory requirements and the responsibilities they may have so that compliance deficiencies can be recognised. There are also specific training requirements which must be met by drivers of vehicles used to transport radioactive materials; these are set out in the Carriage of Dangerous Goods by Road (Driver Training) Regulations 1996. HSE has responsibility for the enforcement of these Regulations.[10]

23 The Regulations also require consignors to possess a certificate of approval, for the type of container they plan to use, before they ship a radioactive source for the first time. For shipments originating outside the UK, the DETR must be provided with a copy of the appropriate certificate of approval. In certain cases prior notification of the competent authority may be required whenever a radioactive material is moved offsite.

24 Consignors have the primary responsibility for ensuring the safety of shipments but carriers also have responsibilities, for transit safety and for implementing contingency plans in the event of accidents. For

consignments shipped from overseas, the shipping agent will usually become the consignor from the port of entry and should ensure, among other things, that the carrier can transport the consignment safely and is prepared to respond to transit incidents.

25 At some stage in the delivery of a consignment of radioactive material there will be a transfer of responsibility from the consignor to the consignee. There may also be a transfer from one mode of transport to another which is not entirely within the control of the consignor (eg for imported shipments). In such circumstances, co-operation between employers to ensure the smooth working of these transfers and to maintain the chain of responsibility at all stages is necessary and is a requirement of regulation 4 of the IRR85.

ADMINISTRATIVE ARRANGEMENTS

Notification

26 Employers must notify their local HSE office of their intention to start work with ionising radiations (IRR85 regulation 5 and Schedule 4) at least 28 days before they do so. Office addresses are in local telephone directories. This is the employer's responsibility and does not fall to the local authority or any other agency that is notified.

Radiation protection advisers (RPAs)

27 Radiation protection advisers must be appointed by employers who designate controlled areas in their workplace which people enter or whose employees are exposed to instantaneous dose rates which exceed $7.5\mu Sv.h^{-1}$ (IRR85 regulation 10). A RPA is also required for critical examination of newly commissioned plants (IRR85 regulation 32(2)).

28 For many irradiation plants, it is possible to make a case for not appointing a RPA on the grounds that instantaneous dose rates are well below $7.5\mu Sv.h^{-1}$ and that personal access during normal source or generator exposure is physically impossible (excluding source change operations), thereby obviating the need to designate a controlled area. However, the radiological hazards presented by most irradiation plants are such that, when certain things go wrong, the potential for life-threatening exposure can be very great indeed. Failure to have appointed a RPA to give advice during and in anticipation of such eventualities would therefore amount to a failure to have done everything reasonably practicable to ensure the safety of people in the workplace. It is therefore good practice to make RPA appointments for all irradiation plants but especially those in Categories II and IV and for source changing operations.

29 As with notification of work with ionising radiation, HSE must be given 28 days notice of RPA appointments. However, because of the need to consider in detail all aspects of the safety of the facility, it is advisable to make these appointments as early as possible in planning and construction work.

30 The RPA should be suitably experienced and qualified to give advice on the radiation safety of irradiators. In particular the RPA should have:

(a) a thorough knowledge of the ionising radiation hazards associated with irradiation plants, so that advice on effective risk assessment and identification of control measures can be given, and an understanding of the control and interlocking techniques available to address such hazards;

(b) general knowledge of the industrial irradiation industry, including the market it operates in and its typical working practices, so that the working practices of the employer who appoints the RPA can be assessed within their proper context and so that meaningful advice on radiation safety matters can be given;

(c) a detailed working knowledge of occupational health and safety law relating to irradiators, to include all relevant statutory provisions, approved codes of practice and guidance documents;

(d) the ability to give advice on how to meet legal requirements and adopt good radiation safety practice; and

(e) skills in communication so that radiation safety issues can be conveyed to all levels of management.

31 IRR85 ACOP, paragraphs 68 to 76 give more information about RPA appointment[2] and the matters on which employers should seek advice. Chief among these is the employer's need to obtain advice on training and information provision to staff when a new irradiation facility is being planned.

Training

32 Staff should receive training and instruction which enables them to conduct their work in accordance with the Regulations (IRR85, regulation 12). The following topics should be included in training programmes:

(a) radiation hazards and health effects;

(b) radiation protection techniques, eg shielding, distance and time;

(c) how to use radiation measuring equipment, eg dose rate meters, installed alarms and electronic personal dosemeters;

(d) plant safety control systems, their purpose and operation;

(e) safe working practices for the plant; and

(f) emergency arrangements.

33 It is good practice to give refresher training annually and whenever staff changes occur. The RPA should be consulted on how best to set up and run training programmes for employees. It is also good practice to involve appointed safety representatives and, where appropriate, any established safety committee in the development and operation of training schemes.

34 The manufacturer or supplier of the plant should be consulted when training programmes are being developed and especially when training of staff takes place during plant commissioning .

35 Prior to commissioning, plant managers will need extensive training in all aspects of the plant's operation so that appropriate systems of work can be established. The RPA, manufacturer or supplier of the plant will have important roles in this.

Radioactive substance control

36 Radioactive substance control has two aspects: restriction of external radiation exposure and contamination control. Contamination control is not a problem in most circumstances of irradiation plant operation because the sources employed are sealed in high-integrity encapsulations which comply with international standards. Plant operators should nonetheless know to what performance standards their sources are constructed. They should ensure that sources comply with the requirements of BS 5288[11] or an equivalent standard. In particular the law requires employers to:

(a) where appropriate, check sources for leakage at least every 26 months (IRR85, regulation 18(3));

(b) use radiation monitoring to confirm the effectiveness of exposure restriction controls around designated areas (IRR85 regulation 24(1));

(c) ensure that radioactive sources are stored safely (IRR85 regulation 20(1)); and

(d) keep up-to-date records of the quantity and location of all radioactive sources used in the workplace and keep such records for at least two years after source disposal (IRR85 regulation 19).

Classification of workers and medical surveillance

Who should be classified?

37 In routine operation, irradiators do not cause personal radiation exposure and personnel who operate them would not normally be required to be classified persons (IRR85 regulation 9). However, given the extremely high dose rates typically produced in irradiators, it is good practice to provide all workers with some form of personal dosimetry so that if an incident occurs, dose control measures can be implemented.

38 Personal dosimetry also provides a way of retrospectively checking that all is well at the plant and gives early indication of incipient failures in engineered controls and problems with systems of work. Personal indicating dosemeters, such as electronic and quartz fibre electroscope (QFE) devices, are also useful as a means of immediately alerting personnel to the unexpected dose rates that might occur during plant faults.

39 Many employers decide that their personal dosimetry needs are such that worker safety assurance is improved if they decide to classify their workers and, as a general rule, this should always happen where significant radiation exposure is a real possibility. For example, employers who do their own maintenance or source changing should classify their workers.

40 There are some circumstances where designation of classified persons is good practice even though it remains unlikely that personal exposures will exceed three-tenths of the relevant dose limit. For example, it would be bad practice to use written systems of work in place of worker classification for employees who routinely enter irradiator chambers throughout their working day. The RPA should always be consulted about the appropriateness of worker classification in particular work circumstances.

41 When workers are classified, the employer has additional responsibilities. These include arranging pre-employment medical examination, medical surveillance (IRR85 regulation 16), regular dose assessment and arrangements for keeping dose records (IRR85 regulation 13). The employer must arrange for an approved dosimetry service (ADS) and an appointed doctor to provide these services. It is also important that the employer ensures that dosemeters are properly worn by employees and that they are returned promptly to the ADS as required.

Area designations

42 Areas where significant personal exposure risks exist must be identified so that entry to those which can cause personal exposure above three-tenths of any dose limit can be restricted by physical demarcation and the use of barriers (IRR85, regulation 8). Such locations are required to be designated as *Controlled Areas* and must be described in local rules.

43 Areas where personal exposures cannot exceed three-tenths but can exceed one-tenth of any dose limit must be designated as *Supervised Areas* and must also be described in local rules.

44 Irradiaton plants seldom have work areas that, in the normal course of events, need to be designated as Controlled Areas. This is because their design includes safety-interlocked exposure controls which make personal access to the source or generator at dose rates in excess of $7.5\mu Sv.h^{-1}$ an event which cannot normally occur (IRR85 regulation 8). However, significant personal exposure risks may arise in the event of a plant fault or from lapses in systems of work and so it is good practice to designate irradiation chambers as Controlled Areas (IRR85 regulation 8(3)). Notwithstanding these considerations, Controlled Areas should always be set up during maintenance and source changing procedures.

Monitoring radiation

45 Employers must ensure that levels of radiation in and around the Controlled and Supervised Areas they designate are properly assessed so that the effectiveness of exposure restriction controls can be monitored (IRR85 regulation 24). The equipment used to do this monitoring must be suitable for measuring the type of radiation at the plant and it must be properly calibrated and maintained by a qualified person. For example, employers need to consider the maximum dose rate which monitoring equipment might reasonably encounter, so that it can be tested up to, or beyond, such dose rates.

46 Advice on monitoring equipment provision, maintenance and testing is given in booklet HSG49.[12]

47 It is good practice to provide a small radioactive test source at the entrance to irradiator chambers so that the operation of hand-held monitors can be checked before entry. However, care must be taken to ensure that the test source is not in such a position that it continues to give a reading on the monitor when an entry is made; over time this could lead to complacency about the meaning of such readings and a dangerous situation could then be overlooked. It is also essential that hand-held monitors used for this purpose are capable of giving meaningful dose rate indications when sources are exposed or generators switched on; many hand-held monitors fail to indicate any dose rate when exposed to the very large radiation fields present in irradiator chambers, and so it is important to select equipment which will be suitable.

Critical examinations

48 The dose restriction and safety features of a new irradiator plant must be critically examined under the supervision of an RPA (IRR85 regulation 32(2)) appointed by either the plant installer or the employer who will operate it. This should be done before the plant is brought into service.

49 The examination should involve a full radiation survey around the exposure cell or chamber so that any radiation leaks are identified. The data obtained in the survey should be filed so that future survey data, required by IRR85 regulation 24, can be properly assessed. The IRR85 ACOP[2] deals with these requirements in more detail.

50 The critical examination should confirm the following key points:

(a) that safety interlocks and warning devices operate properly; and

(b) that there is adequate source or generator shielding.

51 Hand-over documentation should also be prepared by the manufacturer/supplier in consultation with the RPA. This should deal with all aspects of the irradiator's use and maintenance and should contain the information the plant-operating employer needs to comply with the law.

SAFETY ASSESSMENT

What the law requires

52 All employers have a general duty under the Management of Health and Safety at Work Regulations 1992[13] to carry out a risk assessment of their work activities so that the measures needed to comply with the requirements and prohibitions imposed on them by or under relevant statutory provisions can be identified.

53 For work with ionising radiation, this assessment needs to identify the things the employer must do to meet the requirements of IRR85, in particular regulations 6 and 27. The assessment should also deal with the hazard assessment requirements of regulation 25. Guidance on the matters which need to be addressed can be found in Part I and Part II, section 6 of the IRR85 ACOP.[2]

54 The overriding objective of the assessment should be identification of what needs to be done to restrict, so far as is reasonably practicable, personal exposure to radiation in normal operation and following reasonably foreseeable incidents.

55 Special hazard assessments required under IRR85 regulation 26 are not normally necessary for irradiators because most meet either of the following requirements:

(a) the quantity of radioactive material does not exceed that shown in IRR85, schedule 2, column 6 (for Cobalt-60 the limit is 2×10^{12} Bq); or

(b) the sealed source complies with the specification requirements set out in IRR85, schedule 9.

56 Employers should consult their RPA and the irradiator manufacturer/supplier about the need for special hazard assessments.

57 The following paragraphs give guidance on what it is good practice to include in an irradiator safety assessment.

General principles

58 Irradiator safety assessment is a complex task and employers should always consult their RPA for advice. RPA consultation is particularly important for assessments made under IRR85 regulation 25.

59 In the case of Category II and IV irradiators, employers (especially suppliers, manufacturers and installers) should also consider their need to consult a specialist in safety-critical control systems in order to ensure that their assessment covers all aspects of irradiator operation. In this regard, it is good practice to use risk analysis techniques such as *probabilistic safety analysis* (PSA). An example of these techniques is given in the Appendix.

60 Safety assessment findings should be recorded and kept up-to-date.

What should the assessment cover?

61 Hazards associated with all operational conditions need to be included, ie:

(a) routine operation of the plant;

(b) routine maintenance, such as servicing;

(c) repair;

(d) source changing;

(e) plant modification; and

(f) accident or emergency situations.

62 Human factors such as operator error, deliberate acts to undermine safety systems and responses by people to incidents also need to be considered. Most irradiator incidents which have been reported world-wide have been caused, at least in part, by human factors and so it is vitally important that these issues are properly addressed.

63 Assessment needs should be discussed by managers and operators together with safety representatives and any established safety committee. This will ensure that safety-critical points about the plant's design and the way in which people actually operate it are not overlooked. Discussion will also enable effective systems of work to be established.

64 Initially, all operational contingencies, however unlikely or bizarre, should be included in safety assessments. This is the best way of ensuring that nothing is missed. Once the risks associated with a contingency have been established, decisions about the need do anything about it can be made.

LOCAL RULES AND CONTINGENCY PLANNING

65 Written local rules are required for all work with ionising radiation (IRR85 regulation 11(1)); they should describe how work with ionising radiation at the employer's premises is to comply with IRR85. Employers must also ensure that their work with ionising radiation is supervised to the extent required by IRR85; in particular, they must ensure that relevant local rules are observed.

66 It is good practice to involve the RPA, appointed safety representative and, where appropriate, any established safety committee[14,15] in the development and supervision of local rules and contingency plans: they work best when all parties feel that they have a stake in their development and application in the workplace.

67 It is good practice to ensure that local rules properly describe an area's access restrictions and arrangements for dealing with incidents; they should also name those who have management responsibilities in such situations. Local rules should also describe the systems of work to be used for planned and unplanned maintenance and for source leakage testing.

68 It is extremely important that local rules fully describe correct cell entry procedures as a step-by-step list. In particular, the list should cover the operator's need to use a hand-held radiation meter or personal indicating dosemeter, capable of giving audible warnings, whenever the irradiator/chamber is entered; it is good practice to issue personnel with both types of instrument. Such provision is cheap, simple to implement and has been shown to save lives. It ensures that operators are warned of any radiation inside an irradiation chamber, such as might arise if safety interlocks and source return or generator exposure termination mechanisms completely fail.

Scope of contingency planning

69 Employers must prepare contingency plans (IRR85 regulation 27) for all reasonably foreseeable accidents and incidents which could cause personal radiation exposure above relevant dose limits or which could make it necessary to set up new controlled areas or to extend existing ones. The following paragraphs give general advice on some of the issues that may need to be addressed when preparing a suitable plan.

70 The plan should set out the ways in which the employer will continue to restrict radiation exposures when accidents occur, so far as is reasonably practicable. It should address the possibility of accidents arising both during routine plant operation and during non-routine work such as source changing, leakage testing and plant repair and modification.

71 Contingency plans should cover the involvement, if any, of emergency services, hospitals, medical advisers and the irradiator manufacturer or supplier; employers will therefore need to consult these parties when preparing them. Contingency plans should also be reviewed regularly so that they can take account of changes in plant operation and staffing, particularly in relation to safety appointments. They should always be written and all staff should be trained in how to implement them effectively.

72 The need for periodic contingency plan rehearsals to ensure that they will work when needed should always be considered. Plans which involve parties other than just the employer should always be periodically rehearsed. When considering the need for rehearsals, employers need to think not just about the severity of the accident the plan is designed to control but also about the difficulties those who have to implement it may have. People's memories are short and therefore complex plans will need to be practised regardless of the scale of the incident being catered for.

73 Employers should consider splitting contingency plans into a number of parts so that employees can be given just the information they need to respond to an emergency. However, employees should still know something of the overall strategy of control in any

particular incident situation. For example it is often possible to split contingency plans into separate sections dealing with accidents arising from:

(a) routine operation of the plant;

(b) plant maintenance; or

(c) source changes.

74 Contingency plans prepared in this way should be cross-referenced so that their parts can be co-ordinated.

75 People with specific responsibilities should be identified and their role properly described. They should be adequately trained in how to operate the parts of the plan which apply to them.

76 Contingency plans should specifically deal with the following points:

(a) How to recognise operational problems, raise the alarm and make initial responses to an emergency. For example, information about warning signals which indicate that a problem has, or may have, arisen needs to be provided.

(b) The immediate actions necessary to secure the safety of workers and other persons, eg area evacuation, incident appraisal and management notification.

(c) The need for calm appraisal of the situation so that an incident's severity and nature can be determined. So often the wrong decisions are made in the early stages of an incident because people jump to conclusions about what has happened. Those who will have to manage an incident will need to know how to get information about the plant's status and what to look for. They will also need to be skilled at de-briefing workers who were eye-witnesses to initial events so that the true nature of the problem can be established. The plan should contain detailed information about normal radiological conditions around the plant so that an incident's nature and severity can be established quickly.

(d) Once the nature of an incident has been established, the plan will then need to provide information about the measures necessary to bring the situation under control or to stop it getting any worse. Radiological monitoring will be important at this stage of contingency plan operation as will the need to set up personnel exclusion zones and warning notices. Workers involved in dealing with an emergency are people under pressure and so the contingency plan should provide them with information about the remedial action necessary for each accident scenario in a clear and succinct way. This will ensure that there can be no confusion about what remedial action is required. Remember too that an incident not dealt with in the contingency plan is always a possibility, so make sure that the plan has something to say about the sort of remedial action to take when a totally unforeseen incident occurs.

(e) Make sure that all responsible persons such as the RPA and RPS and external contact addresses and telephone numbers are included in the plan and that they are kept up-to-date. Sources of advice and assistance should also be listed, for example the regulatory and emergency authorities.

(f) It is good management practice for the employer to appoint a single person to carry out the task of informing the authorities and/or answering enquiries from the press and public. This will ensure that information about the emergency is dealt with consistently.

(g) Make sure that the plan gives information about where to find equipment such as source transport containers, additional monitoring equipment and special tools. Contingency plan rehearsals should include checks for the availability of this emergency equipment.

(h) Incident control is about prevention as well as mitigation. Contingency plans therefore need to include information on how all events and remedial actions should be logged. This information is important to the ongoing management of an incident and to follow-up enquiries made to identify what needs to be done to avoid future similar occurrences.

Liaison with external bodies

77 Contingency plans which rely on help from external bodies such as the emergency services or the source supplier (eg emergency transport containers) should take account of their response times and availability. Effective liaison with all external bodies needed to bring the plan into effect is the only way to ensure that the required services will be available when they are needed.

78 Contingency plans for irradiators which use quantities of radioactive materials exceeding the values given in IRR85, schedule 2, column 6 must be sent to HSE before the radioactive source is brought onto the employer's premises.

REVIEWING ASSESSMENTS AND CONTINGENCY PLANS

79 It is good practice to review hazard assessments and contingency plans at least every two years or whenever there are significant changes to either the irradiator plant itself or its operational procedures. The RPA, appointed safety representative and, where appropriate, any established safety committee[14,15] should be involved in completing these reviews.

Incident prevention

80 Incident prevention depends on a number of factors, the most significant of which are:

(a) safety-related control system performance, eg irradiator entry interlocks;

(b) staff training and competence;

(c) the effectiveness of inspection regimes in highlighting incipient faults; and

(d) effective preventative maintenance.

81 It is good practice to keep records of near-miss events so that the circumstances which led to them can be avoided. Operational records also assist in the analysis of plant performance and help to reveal trends which could lead to an incident. When records of plant performance or safety indicate that changes to operational procedures or plant design are needed, the employer should ensure that both the hazard assessment and contingency plan are updated accordingly.

82 Examples of incidents which should be recorded and which would require immediate investigation are:

(a) stuck source problems involving its failure to return to the storage location;

(b) fires and explosions inside irradiator chambers;

(c) source frame damage;

(d) failure of source hoist cables or transit mechanisms;

(e) irradiation chamber access problems;

(f) radioactively contaminated product;

(g) spurious alarms and interlock actuation;

(h) contamination outside the cell;

(i) radiation damage of electrical insulation within the irradiation chamber;

(j) in the case of wet source store irradiators, storage pool liner or pipework damage; abnormal storage pool water loss; storage pool water chemistry changes and radioactive contamination of storage pool water.

SAFETY ASSURANCE

83 Irradiator manufacturers and suppliers should provide comprehensive information about safety systems fitted to their equipment. Employers will need this information in order to operate the irradiator safely. IRR85 ACOP, Part II, section 6 gives information on the sort of control systems which should be installed.

84 To achieve safe operation, complex devices such as irradiators use safety-related control systems (SRCS). To work effectively, an SRCS should be both functionally and, where practicable, physically independent from other irradiator control systems. This ensures that, when an incident occurs, the SRCS remains effective.

85 An SRCS needs to have two features: it should make it impossible for a person to gain access to the irradiator source or generator when in the exposed position or switched on, and it should be fault tolerant.

86 Engineered exposure control is achieved by interlocking source and generator exposure mechanisms with the points of entry to the exposure chamber so that they remain locked while the source/generator is exposed or switched on. For example, this can be achieved by having a mechanical device at irradiator entrance doors or lids which directly disables the source or generator exposure mechanism. Interlocking can also be achieved by an electrical 'logic' system which makes decisions about irradiator status from the inputs received from control devices such as source rack position detectors, door closure detectors and in-cell radiation detectors. Principles for design and selection of interlocking devices are described in safety standard BS EN 1088.[16]

87 Electrical techniques are more flexible than mechanical designs and are often preferred by designers and manufacturers nowadays. But they can be more difficult to make fail-safe than mechanical safety interlocks. With the advent of software-driven programmable controllers, particularly in relation to Category II and IV irradiators, the issue of fault tolerance and mitigation in the SRCS has become vitally important to overall safety assurance.

88 A complete discussion of SRCS design and implementation is beyond the scope of this guidance. More information on this topic is available in HSE guidance on programmable electronic systems (PES).[17]

89 Irradiator safety assurance depends on the use of one or all of the following design principles:

(a) **Inherent safety (fail-safety and fault tolerance)**
Here, individual components within a SRCS are designed to have no safety-critical consequences when they fail. The simplest example of this principle is electrical design which ensures that failures in relays and devices such as door closure detection switches do not cause hazardous conditions in themselves or render the SCRS incapable of detecting a hazardous condition in the irradiator system(s) it is designed to protect.

(b) **Redundancy and diversity**
When risk assessment indicates that failure of a component within a SRCS has unavoidable safety-critical consequences, designers have to consider ways of providing a backup component which has a similar function. SRCSs which have such backup systems are said to have 'redundancy'. Ideally, backup devices should operate quite differently from the 'primary' system they are designed to protect, a design approach referred to as 'diversity'.

An SRCS which unlocks irradiation chamber entrance doors only when in-cell radiation detectors signal the absence of significant dose rates and when either a 'source return to store' or, in the case of generators, a 'power off ' signal has been received, has both diversity and redundancy. This design principle is widely adopted in Category II and IV irradiators but often the fail-safety of the controller that processes the signals from safety devices such as in-cell detectors is overlooked in risk analysis.

Irradiator designers need to pay particular attention to this issue if they are to build plant with the necessary level of safety integrity. Safety Standard IEC 61508[18] gives information about safety integrity and defines it as the 'probability of a safety-related system satisfactorily performing the required safety functions under all the stated conditions within a stated period of time'.

Redundancy and diversity do not just apply to engineered features; administrative arrangements can also be involved. For example, a system of work which requires workers to have a radiation monitor with them when they enter an irradiation cell will provide protection when engineered systems fail. However, remember that administrative arrangements are less reliable than engineered controls; they should never be used as the primary means of safety assurance.

(c) **Safety integrity (safety function reliability)**
This approach is seldom used in the design and construction of irradiators mainly because methods (a) and (b) are more cost-effective. Safety assurance by the use of high-safety integrity components in the SRCS requires three things: quality-assured design and fabrication to an acceptable level of safety performance, quality-assured in-service maintenance, and extensive data on component failure mode probabilities so that operational life can be determined. The problem with the safety integrity approach is that there has to be a consensus on acceptable levels of failure probability and so far as public opinion is concerned, this is not always easy to establish.

The aviation industry is a good example of these principles in operation. Here, when redundancy cannot be used, quality-assured safety integrity is used instead. For example, aircraft engines can be replicated to provide redundancy but the turbine blades in each, which if they fail could endanger the whole aircraft, have to be guaranteed to operate at an acceptable level of safety integrity.

90 The following examples illustrate the ways in which these three safety assurance principles are applied specifically to the design and operation of irradiators:

(a) **Inherent safety**
Irradiators cannot be designed to be wholly inherently safe; 'redundancy' and 'safety integrity' are also necessary to the overall safety assurance of any particular design. However, where practicable the inherent safety approach is the preferred option. The following are some examples of SRCS components being used in this way:

(i) Door closure switches designed and installed so that when they fail, following return spring failure or poor electrical connection for example, the source or generator exposure mechanism remains disabled.

(ii) In-cell radiation detectors fitted with priming sources so that a detectable output signal is always produced. This technique enables the control circuit to detect immediately any failure in the detector's sensitivity to radiation.

(iii) Making use of gravity in source exposure mechanism design so that when the mechanism fails, the source falls back to the storage position automatically.

(b) **Redundancy**
Making use of a number of control devices, each operating in a different way, to interlock source or generator exposure mechanisms with irradiation chamber personal access points is good irradiator design practice. Interlocking can be achieved by mechanical and/or electrical means and may involve a controller that is software programmable. Examples of control devices include door closure switches and electromechanical locks, in-cell radiation detectors, source position detectors and search and lock-up devices. IRR85, ACOP Part II section 6 gives more information on the types of devices which are typically needed.

(c) **Safety integrity**
Source encapsulation performance, throughout its life in the irradiator, is critical to overall plant safety integrity assurance. Sources are designed to meet stringent international containment standards so that, in normal use, they do not leak radioactivity. This is achieved by double encapsulation of the radioactive material and rigorous quality assurance checks during manufacture. Irradiation sources are also designed to meet stringent leakage requirements during foreseeable accidents such as fire.

Safety critical system components such as in-cell gamma radiation detectors and interlock devices are normally designed to have very high safety integrity throughout their design life. It is therefore important that the design life of such components is established by plant designers and manufacturers and made known to those who will have responsibility for their maintenance. This enables replacement schedules for time-expired components to be established so that overall plant safety integrity can be assured.

91 It is good practice to discontinue irradiator operations whenever a redundant safety system fails. Redundancy is not about providing back-up systems which allow an irradiator to continue to be operated during a fault but rather it is about operating the plant to a guaranteed level of safety assurance.

92 Detailed advice on all of the above matters, particularly on electrical control systems, is contained in BS EN 60204-1.[19]

Programmable electronic systems

93 Programmable systems have become very important in all manner of process control applications in recent years. They bring unparalleled flexibility and safety integrity to manufacturing and materials processing but also unique problems. The complexity of programmable devices such as microprocessors and of software means that it is not possible to predict all the ways in which such systems could fail: their use in safety-related control systems therefore has to take account of this weakness.

94 As a general rule, the consequences to irradiator safety of erroneous programmable controller 'decisions' need to be addressed at the design stage. All possible failure modes need to be identified so that provision can be made to either mitigate their safety consequences or prevent their occurrence.

95 Mitigation involves the use of redundancy in the function affected by a fault so that it continues to be provided; programmable controller and software replication are examples of this technique. Prevention involves the use of hazard analysis to determine the specification, design, testing and maintenance needed to ensure that software and hardware performance meet a specified level of safety integrity.

96 A combination of these two approaches is needed in order to build programmable devices which have a high level of overall safety integrity.

97 Programmable controllers should not be able to be re-programmed by anyone other than the manufacturer or a suitably trained maintenance engineer. It is particularly important that operators are fully trained in how to use the systems installed at the plant at which they work. The manufacturer must fully inform the user of the significance of any changes made to programmable controllers, for example changes made following maintenance and repair work.

98 Most systems allow interlocks to be disabled so that some types of maintenance can be completed and so that emergencies can be dealt with, but such actions should be very strictly supervised and preferably subject to a permit-to-work system. Interlock disablement should also be under dual key control. Further information on programmable controllers is available in HSE guidance *Programmable electronic systems in safety-related applications.*[17]

OTHER SAFETY ISSUES

Purchasing radioactive sources

99 When placing a contract for the supply of radioactive sources, it is good practice to discuss with the supplier how they will be delivered and installed in the irradiator. Each party can then ensure that the work is conducted safely. This need for co-operation and consultation is a requirement under IRR85 regulation 4. The irradiator operator and supplier will need to discuss their respective contingency plans and will need to decide who will control the areas where irradiator sources are stored pending their being loaded into the irradiator.

100 The International Transport Regulations require regular maintenance of transport containers. The 'maintenance-due date' must be shown on both the container and consignment documentation. Employers who plan to purchase sources should ensure that delivery and 'spent' source return times are agreed in the contract. This ensures that there is no possibility that a transport container maintenance date will expire while it is at their premises awaiting return to the consignor.

101 IRR85 regulation 18 requires employers to 'ensure that the design, construction and maintenance of any article containing a radioactive substance, including its ... immediate container ... is such as to prevent the leakage of any radioactive substance ...' Regulation 18 also requires that, where appropriate, suitable leak tests are carried out at suitable intervals, which in no case should exceed 26 months. Source manufacturers should be consulted on how best to do this. BS 5288, Appendix D[11] describes some suitable test methods and acceptable detection limits. Records of leakage tests must be kept for a period of two years after the date on which they are made.

102 Employers need to consult their supplier about the specification of their sources and obtain the necessary certificates of conformity with relevant source manufacturing standards. Suppliers are required under section 6 of the HSW Act to make this information available to their customers. The information the employer obtains from the supplier should include the following:

(a) that the sources and their encapsulation meet the requirements of IRR85, Schedule 9; and

(b) that adequate leak testing has been carried out prior to shipment of the sources.

Ancillary equipment

103 All equipment not supplied by the manufacturer or supplier of the irradiator but which forms part of an installation, for example conveyors, compressors and hoists, should be safe to use Management of Health and Safety at Work Regulations (MHSW)[20] and Provision and Use of Work Equipment Regulations (PUWER).[21] Employers will need to ensure that risk assessment of this equipment is not overlooked at the time of irradiator installation and commissioning.

104 Lifting equipment safety should also not be neglected. Fork-lift trucks and machinery such as conveyors must comply with relevant regulations and codes of practice[22,23,24,25] and must be regularly tested. Local rules should include systems of work and training requirements for those who work with such equipment.

105 Some Category II and IV irradiation plant use a wire rope to lift the source frame from its storage position to the operating (exposed) position; this will need to be periodically inspected and tested just like any other lifting equipment.

106 Toxic materials and solvents must be stored safely and care should be taken to ensure that no substances are introduced into the irradiation chamber which might chemically degrade under irradiation to produce unexpected toxic or flammable by-products.[26] Irradiator operators should know at all times what is being irradiated so that chemical degradation risks can be assessed and provision made for their control.

107 At wet source store irradiators, the maintenance of storage pond water purity is vitally important because impurities can cause long-term degradation of source encapsulation. Employers should set up regular water quality checks so that the effectiveness of water purification and treatment can be checked.

108 Large-scale irradiators require forced ventilation to remove gases such as ozone produced when air and the product are irradiated. Other noxious gases such as nitrogen oxides may be liberated too. Irradiator manufacturers and suppliers normally incorporate a ventilation system into their designs but employers will usually have the responsibility for managing the discharge of these gases to the environment. They should make sure that discharge points are located so that there is no possibility of gas being drawn back into the workplace.

109 Ozone is subject to a maximum exposure limit (MEL) under the Control of Substances Hazardous to Health Regulations 1994.[26] Employers who operate irradiators will need to make sure that irradiator chamber entry delay times are long enough to allow the ventilation system to reduce ozone levels to below this limit. Since ozone generation depends upon source or generator size, entry delay times should be modified whenever changes to either are made.

110 Irradiation causes heating which can lead to fire. Category II and IV irradiators should therefore have a fire detection system installed within the irradiation chamber. This should work on either heat or smoke detection. Fire containment is seldom a problem because the shielding needed in irradiators usually provides effective containment. But if a fire starts when a source is in the exposed position, failure of source return mechanisms may occur and the source itself may be damaged. It is therefore good practice to consider the use of an automatic fire extinguishing system. Where it is inappropriate to use water as the extinguishant, the use of a gaseous system should be considered.

111 To minimise accidents in production environments, workplace cleanliness and tidiness are essential. For work with ionising radiation, good workplace house keeping is all the more important. Employers who operate irradiators should strive to promote a disciplined attitude to the work environment.

ELECTRON BEAM DEVICES

112 This section deals with some of the safety issues which are peculiar to electron beam devices. The National Council on Radiation Protection and Measurement (NCRPM) Report No 51[27] gives detailed guidance on radiation protection for such machines. Two examples of such devices are shown in Figures 5 and 6. This section does not cover the use of electron beam devices in welding and cutting applications.

113 Electron beam devices produce ionising radiation in the form of a stream of accelerated electrons. These emerge from an aperture (window) in an evacuated tube into an exposure chamber that may itself be evacuated to improve beam effectiveness and range. Electrons are directly ionising but also cause the emission of X-rays when they strike the product or material being processed. Like gamma devices, electron beam irradiators need to be shielded so that these X-rays do not irradiate workers. However, unlike gamma devices, electron beam irradiators can be turned on and off electrically; source storage devices are therefore not needed and there are no radioactive contamination risks associated with their use. Many of the safety problems mentioned in earlier sections of this guidance therefore do not apply to electron beam irradiators. However, risk assessment is still required in order to ensure safe design and operation.

114 The key difference between electron beam devices and gamma irradiators is in the way in which exposure is initiated. Unlike gamma sources, exposure mechanisms such as shutters and hoists are unnecessary. Safety

interlocking of irradiator entry points is therefore made with the electron beam power supply or emission control system rather than with source hoists etc.

115 Electron beam irradiator safety relies upon the speed and reliability of power supply control systems; these should be designed to work almost instantaneously without causing damage to other components. Power supplies should be interlocked with irradiator chamber human access points in just the same way as source exposure mechanisms are interlocked in gamma irradiators.

116 Unlike gamma irradiators, the radiation output of electron beam devices is alterable. It is therefore important to ensure that only appropriately trained and authorised workers are allowed to make alterations to exposure parameters. Power supply controllers also need to be able to respond to changes in output occurring during faults; this is important for fault conditions which could greatly increase radiation levels in irradiation chambers.

117 To help maintenance engineers and to provide data for ongoing safety assessment, plant operation should be continuously monitored. This enables incidents to be effectively recorded when they occur (see Appendix).

118 Diagnostic equipment should be located at the control panel so that fault finding can be completed by maintenance staff without disabling the main accelerator or bypassing safety interlocks.

119 Irradiation areas which personnel can enter should have highly visible and appropriately labelled emergency beam shut-off switches which are part of the SRCS. Electron beam actuation should be under key control by appropriately authorised and trained operators. Local rules should list the persons so authorised and describe the procedures to be adopted in the event of control key loss.

120 At large irradiators, control circuits for vacuum systems, magnets, DC power to linear accelerator modulators and RF systems etc, are designed to work independently from one another. Each of these auxiliary systems may have its own interlocks and warning devices which may not necessarily form part of the irradiator's overall SRCS. It is therefore important to make clear to operators and especially to maintenance staff, exactly which systems are safety critical. This will ensure that inadvertent and irresponsible safety interlock disablement never occurs.

121 Flashing or rotating warning lights should be provided in all radiation or exclusion areas as well as at the entrances to these areas. These lights should operate automatically, not only when radiation is being produced, but also when the machine controls are set ready to produce radiation. Pre-exposure and exposure warnings should be clearly labelled with signs explaining their significance. Warning systems should also be interlocked with the beam power supply so that it is not possible to run the device with a defective warning light.

122 Irradiators should be fitted with audible and visible warnings which activate whenever radiation levels in areas to which there is personal access increase unexpectedly. In most circumstances these warnings would be produced as soon as any change in background radiation is detected. Warning devices should be interlocked with beam power supplies so that irradiation cannot occur when they are operative.

123 Radiation detectors used in warning systems should be suitable for measurement of the radiation produced by the electron beam device; many devices produce pulsed radiation which might be difficult to measure with conventional equipment. Radiation detectors should also be sensitive to both the electron beam (ie high energy electrons) and X-rays produced by its interaction with the product undergoing irradiation.

124 All electrical circuits and wiring should be carried out in accordance with the Electricity at Work Regulations[28] and associated Memorandum of Guidance.[29]

125 Like gamma irradiators, electron beam devices produce breakdown products which may be noxious or toxic. Electron beam generators themselves may contain hazardous chemicals. For example ancillary equipment, such as high-voltage accelerators, may contain toxic insulating gases such as sulphur-hexafluoride. Storage, transfer, disposal and any maintenance work involving materials such as these will need careful assessment if safety is to be maintained. The irradiator manufacturer or supplier should be consulted about any potentially hazardous materials it may contain so that the requirements of the Control of Substances Hazardous to Health Regulations 1994[26] can be met.

126 Gases, such as nitrogen and carbon dioxide, can be hazardous to personnel if work areas are not well ventilated. Complex gases released following product decomposition and high-voltage arcing in the irradiation area may also be a problem. As with gamma irradiators, ozone and nitrogen oxides production in irradiated air require special attention.

127 Effective control of chemical hazards usually requires the use of forced ventilation within the irradiation area and sometimes in other work areas. During commissioning, measurements should be made of the concentrations of toxic and noxious gases in and around the irradiation chamber. This enables ventilation needs to be determined. Measurements of irradiation chamber clearance times are also needed so that delay times on interlocks can be determined.

128 As with gamma irradiators, electron beam devices are a fire risk; however, there are three phenomena peculiar to their operation which increase this risk:

(a) *Thermal heating effects* - electron beams are highly collimated, intense energy sources capable of producing enormous power densities in target materials. Electron beams have no inherent temperature and so target temperatures are only constrained by their thermal conductivity. For low conductivity materials, ignition temperatures may be reached in just a few seconds; it is therefore important to keep the product moving through the beam. To control this fire risk, product conveyors should be safety interlocked with electron beam power supplies.

Electron beam irradiators should have contingency plans which deal explicitly with fire risks (see paragraph 110) .

(b) *Radiation catalysis* - a number of chemical reactions can be initiated by irradiation and, if sufficiently exothermic, may give rise to fire or explosion.

(c) *Electrical effects of irradiation* - electron beam irradiation causes the product to become electrically charged with an attendant risk of arcing if grounding pathways are not controlled.

129 At beam energies above 6 MeV some target materials, and indeed plant ancillary equipment within the irradiation chamber, can be made radioactive. The RPA should be consulted about this before any high-energy electron beam device is commissioned. Radioisotopes produced in this way are no different from radioactive materials bought for use in the workplace; they need to be controlled and disposed of responsibly and in accordance with the law (IRR85 and RSA 1993).

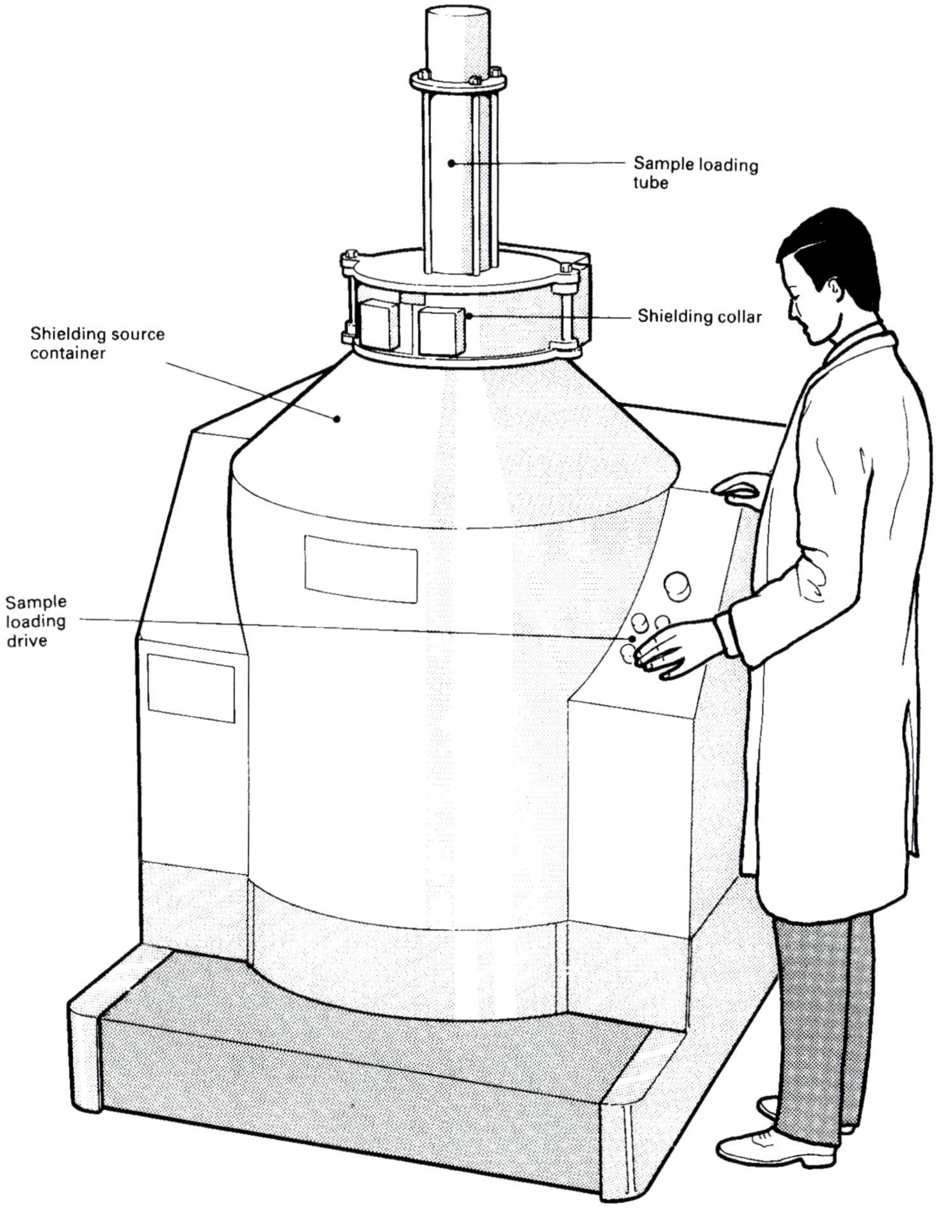

Figure 1 *Self-contained, dry source storage irradiator*

The sealed source is located in a dry container constructed of solid materials. The source is shielded at all times and personal access to the source is physically impossible. This configuration is also applicable to some electron beam irradiators.

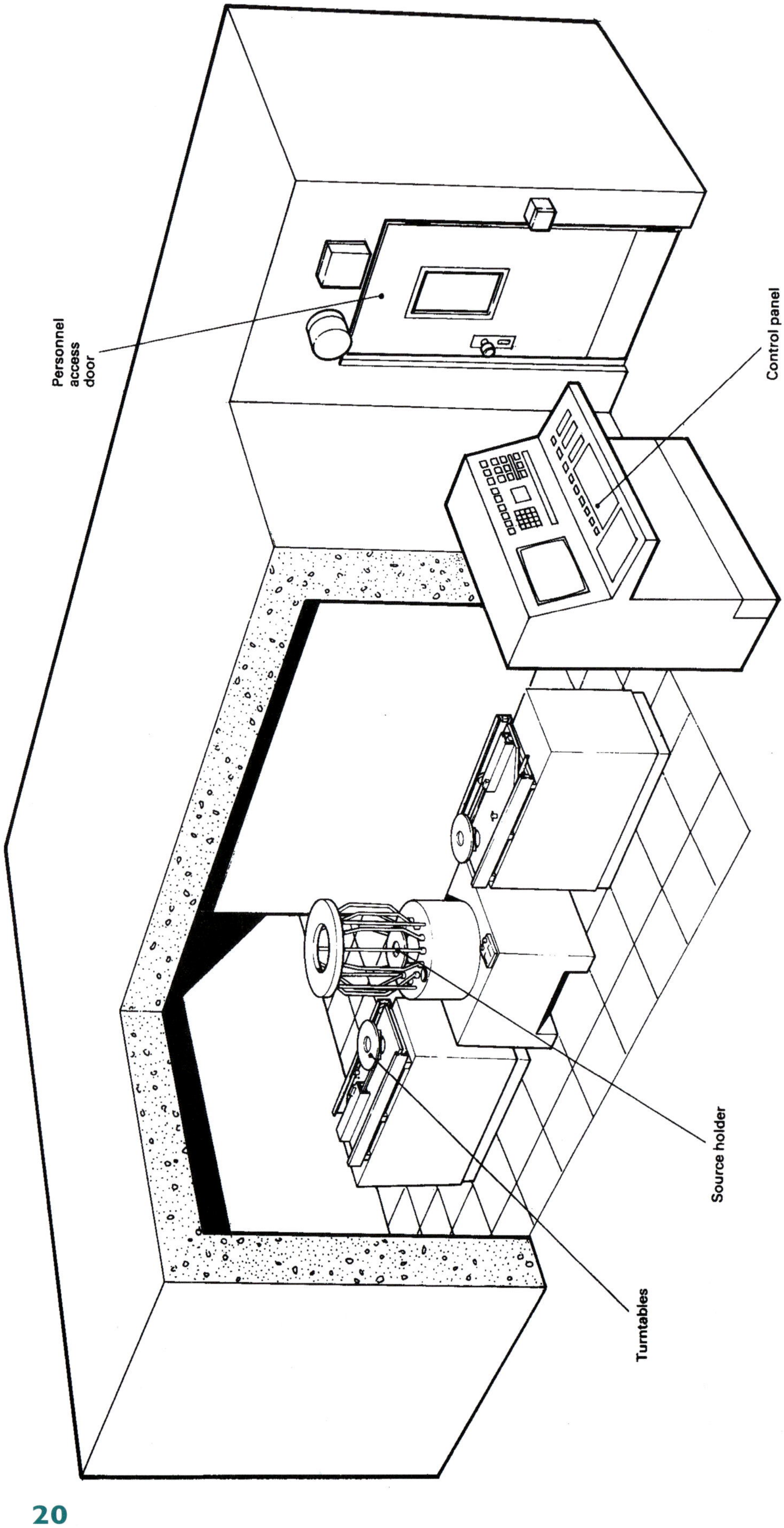

Figure 2 *Panoramic, dry source storage irradiator*

The sealed source is contained in a dry container constructed of solid materials and is fully shielded when not in use. It is exposed within a room which is kept inaccessible during use by an entry control system.

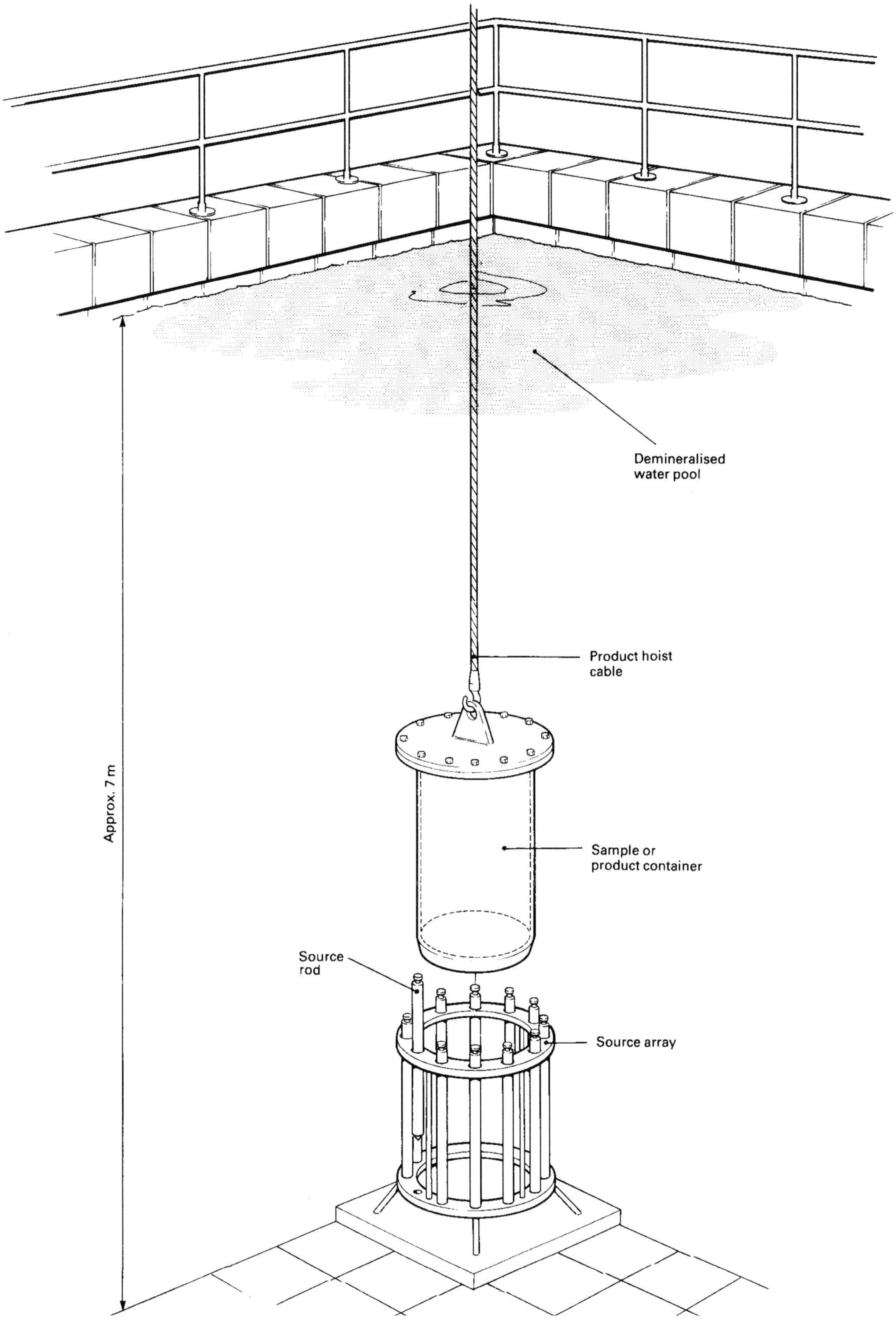

Figure 3 *Self-contained, wet source storage irradiator*

The sealed source is contained in a water-filled storage pool; the source is shielded at all times and personal access to it and to the volume undergoing irradiation is physically prevented.

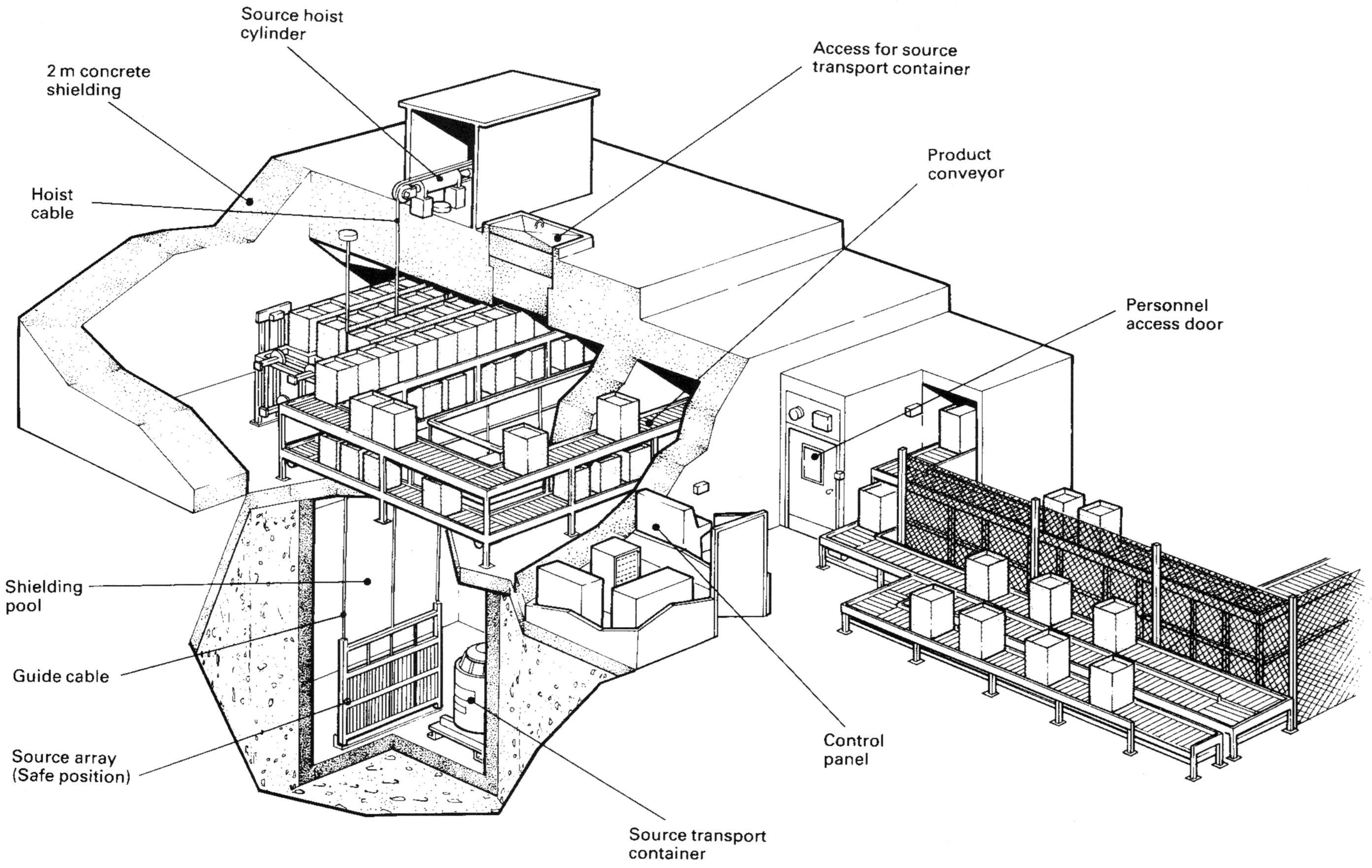

Figure 4 Panoramic, wet source storage irradiator

The sealed source is contained in a water-filled storage pool and is fully shielded when not in use. It can be exposed within a room to which human access is prevented by an entry system.

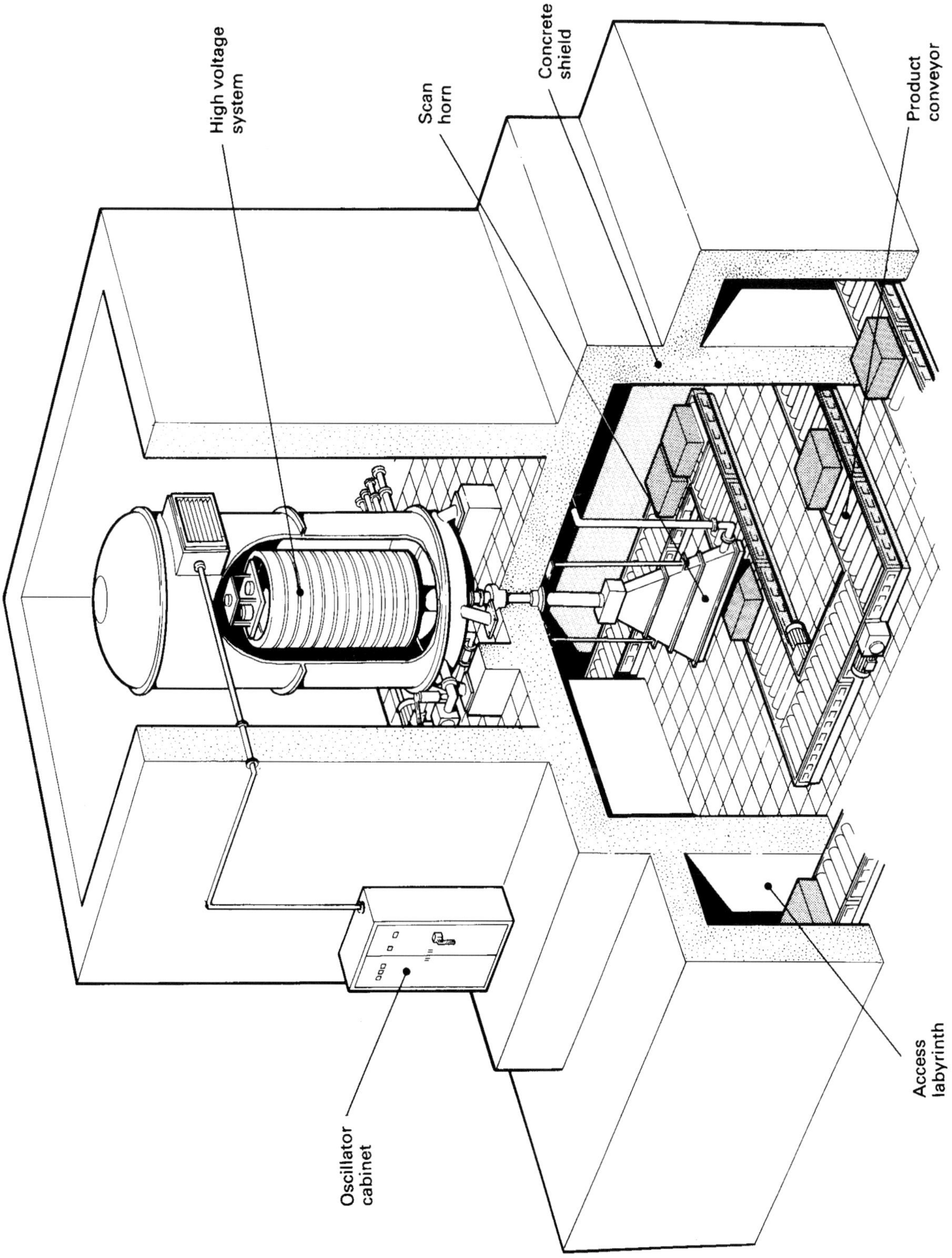

Figure 5 *Electron beam irradiator*

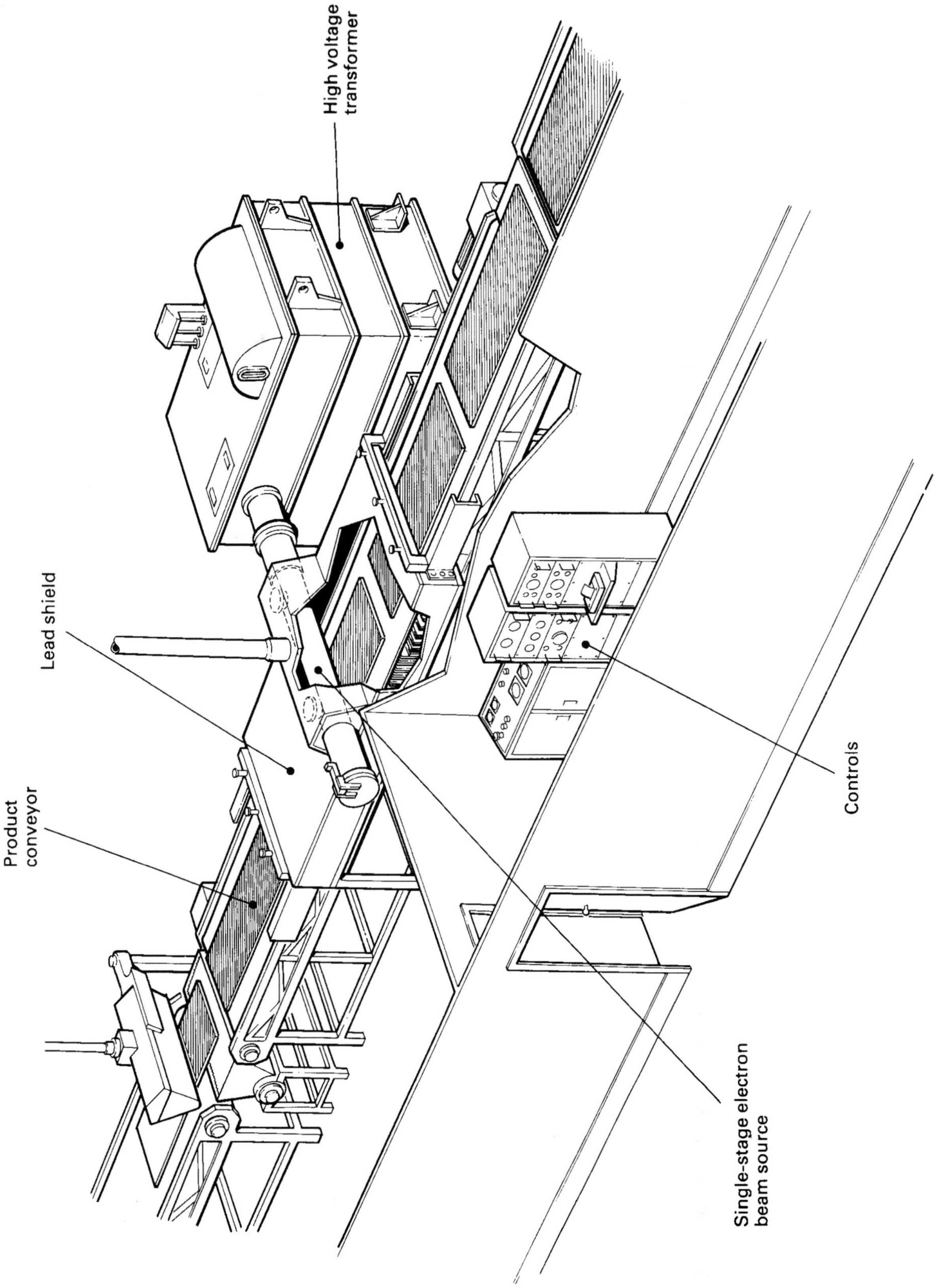

Figure 6 *Self-contained electron beam irradiator*

APPENDIX
PROBABILISTIC SAFETY ASSESSMENT (PSA)

This appendix contains an abridged abstract of a paper published by the International Atomic Energy Agency (IAEA): *Probabilistic safety assessment for large industrial irradiators* IAEA-CS-93H 601 Vienna 1990.[30] It has been modified to make it suitable for use in the safety analysis irradiation plants.

1 PSA is a systematic method of modelling the response of a plant to a set of initiating events which could threaten its safe operation. To develop the necessary models, detailed information about the design and operating principles of the plant is needed. Basic models (such as fault trees or event trees) are developed to identify the possible failure paths. In analysing these models, a number of factors should be taken into account, including the random failure of components, failures arising from some common cause, human errors and deliberate misbehaviour, and operational procedure failures.

Damage state definition

2 Before a model can be set up it is first necessary to define plant damage scenarios and then map out their consequences, for example worker radiation exposure to the source or generator and radioactivity releases which cause radiation exposures and contamination inside or outside the plant. Non-radiological events may also be included in this process such as damage or malfunction of the source frame or hoist which prevents plant operation but does not cause any radiation over-exposure or radioactivity release.

Safety system definition

3 When building the model, plant safety systems and features which should operate following an initiating event need to be identified. For gamma irradiators, these include:

(a) *Source shield* - this may be either the concrete-shielded cell or the water-filled pool inside the cell in which the source frame is stored when in the 'safe' position.

(b) *Safety-related control system* - safety interlock devices and their associated controller which prevent exposure of any person to radiation either by preventing entry to the cell or by automatically removing the source of radiation.

(c) *Fault indicators* - alarms which indicate that a system is not functioning correctly, for example source position indicators, low water-level indicators and smoke and heat detectors.

(d) *Emergency systems* - these are items such as emergency stop devices on control panels, emergency stop devices inside irradiation chambers and emergency escape systems.

(e) *Radiation monitoring* - radiation detectors, such as fixed monitors inside irradiation chambers, portable radiation survey meters, product conveyor exit monitors, storage pond water and ion-exchange resin monitors and personal dosemeters worn by staff.

(f) *Physical barriers* - items which prevent access to irradiation chambers, such as doors, roof plugs, product conveyors, access barriers and mechanical locks.

(g) *Administrative procedures* - written instructions on irradiator use and associated safety requirements (local rules). These instructions identify persons responsible for actions in the event of an incident or accident and describe the procedures to be followed in such situations.

PSA structure

4 The following steps are a guide to carrying out a PSA.

Step 1 Prepare a written description of plant functions, safety features and operational procedures.

Step 2 Identify and list all possible *events* which may create a disturbance to plant operation so that those with a safety consequence can be identified (safety critical events). Make this list as complete as possible. External initiators which could affect the plant should be examined as well as those arising at the plant itself, eg fire and explosion.

Step 3 For each safety-critical *event*, identify the safety functions which are provided to prevent its occurrence or mitigate its consequences.

Step 4 Identify the ways in which the safety functions at *step 3* can fail. These failure modes are the *events* identified in the *event* sequence model. *Fault tree* modelling is the most frequently used technique for this task, but other methods are available.

5 *Type of events* - the identification of accident initiating events is best done by an engineering evaluation based on the operational history of similar plants. These data can be appropriately modified to relate to the particular plant under consideration. The plant supplier should be able to supply this information.

6 *Grouping of events* - events should be grouped so that those which would contribute to a particular type of incident can be identified. Figures 7 and 8 illustrate the types and grouping of possible initiating events for both 'Radiation Exposure' and 'Radioactive Contamination' pathways. Tables 1 and 2 give information on possible failure modes relating to the 'events' described in these figures.

Events can be additionally grouped according to three operating modes:

(a) *normal operation;*

(b) *source handling; and*

(c) *abnormal operation (accident or incident).*

7 *Human failure* - experience has shown that the most serious incidents are caused by personnel behaving irrationally or in a manner contrary to prescribed procedures. The most common problem is plant operation with some or all safety interlocks defeated or removed; this is usually done to make systems of work less onerous. It is essential therefore to examine closely the interlock system insofar as it relates to the actions required of the operator and the extent to which he/she can interfere with its operation. Safety features are usually built into the plant but often they can all too easily be disabled and dismantled by determined individuals. Safety-related control systems should be designed around the practical needs of those who operate the plant so that incentives to interfere with them are minimised.

8 *Normal operating procedures* - normal plant operation analysis should be carried out so that those features which could easily be bypassed by the operator can be improved. The analysis should also identify accident initiators associated with operator negligence or error.

9 *Non-routine operating procedures* - analysis of maintenance and source load/unload activities require careful attention because they are usually performed without normal safety systems being fully operational. It should be possible to design alternative safety

systems which become operational at such times so that these tasks can be performed safely.

10 *PSA report content* - the report needs to be comprehensive but should only include information relevant to safety assurance decision-making. An introduction, outlining the technique used in preparing the report, should be included to assist first-time users who may not be specialists in PSA.

11 All of the above material is covered in much greater depth in the full IAEA report.[30]

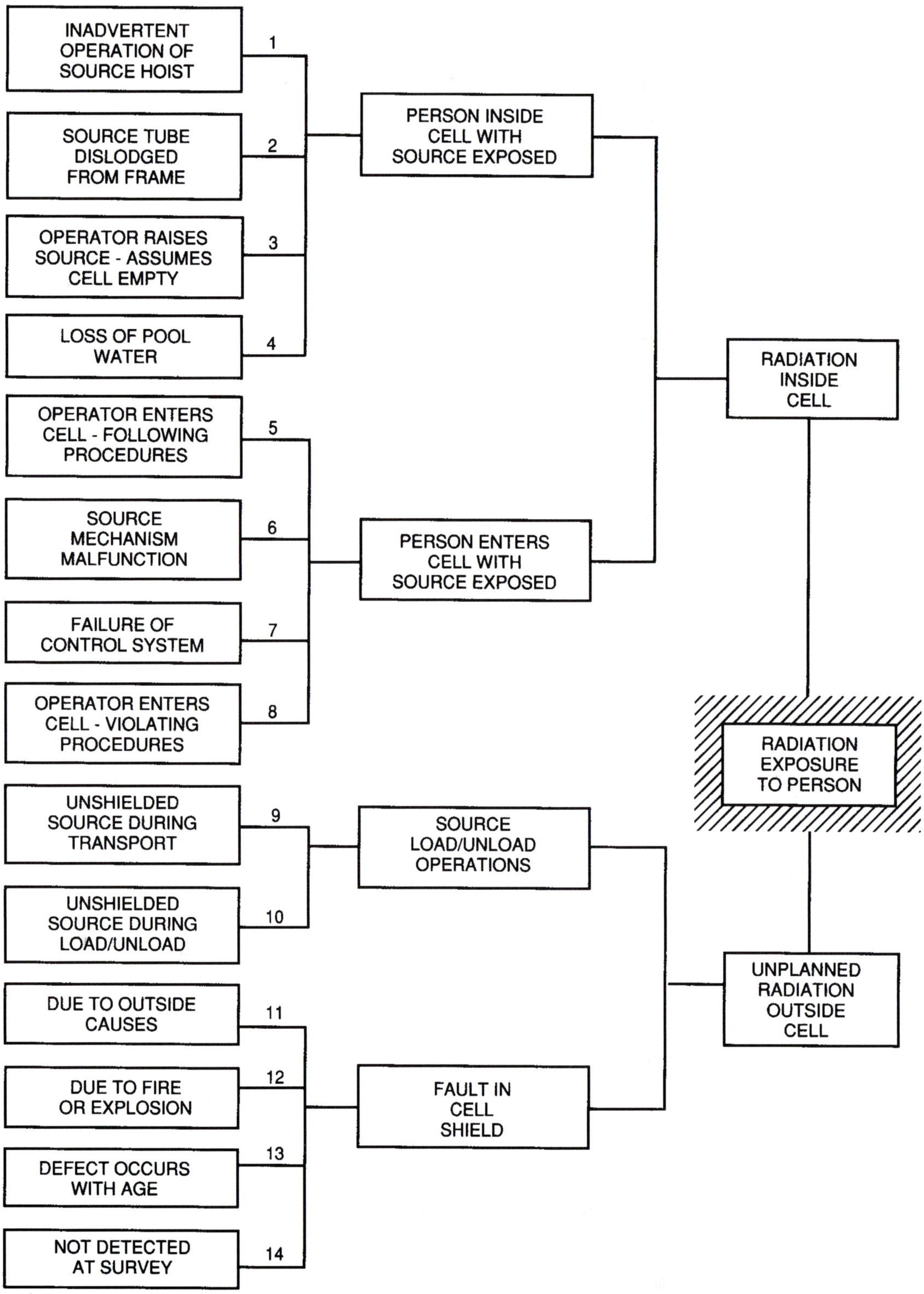

Figure 7 *Events leading to radiation exposure*

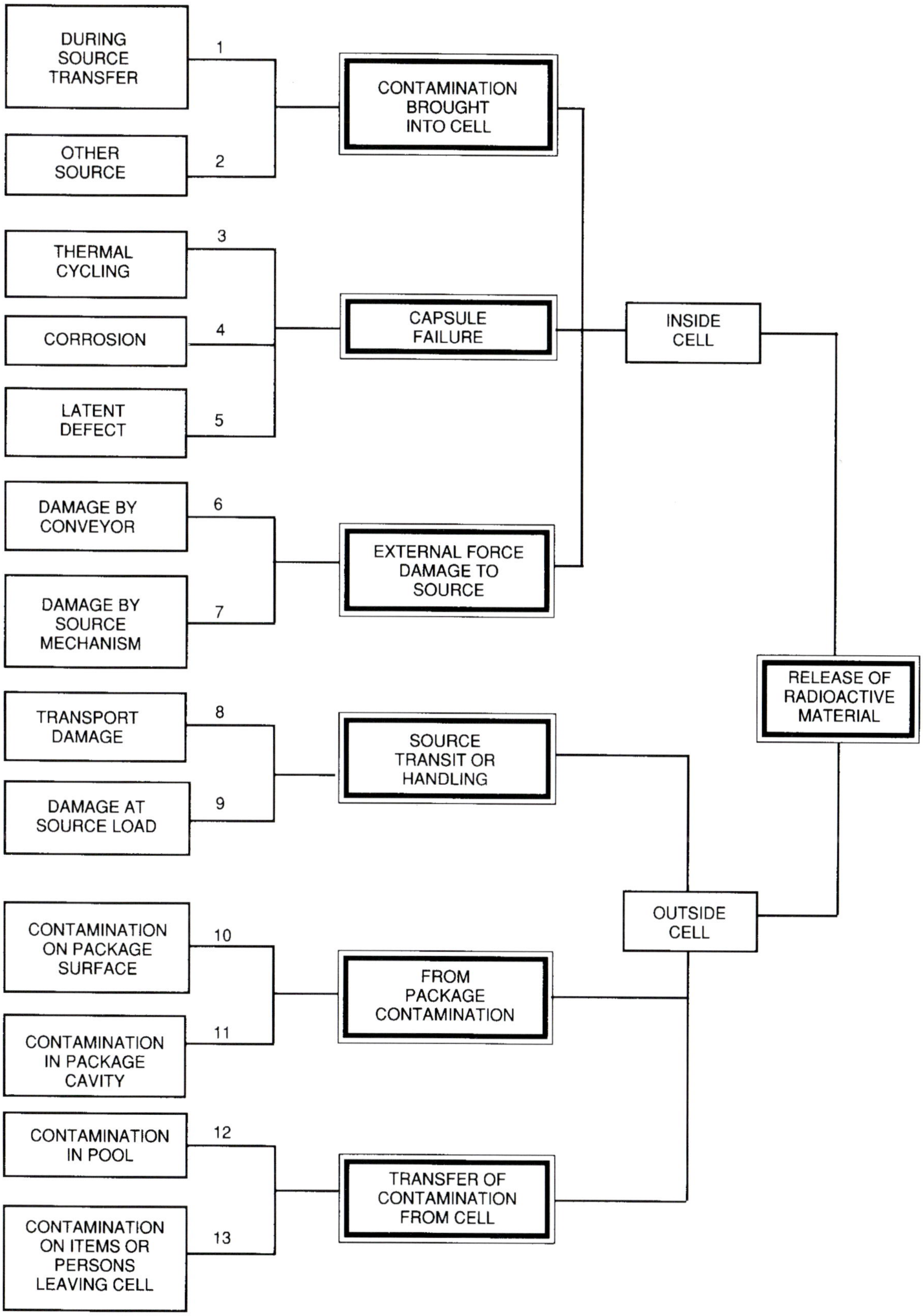

Figure 8 *Events leading to radioactive contamination*

Table 1 Failure modes leading to radiation exposure (event numbers refer to Figure 7)

Event	*Possible failure mode*
1	Interlock failure Control failure Power system failure Mechanical failure Environmental effect on source hoist
2	Caused by mechanical interference Improper source installation Mechanical failure of source frame Failure of source hoist control
3	Person enters of via product gates Person hides in cell Inadequate check of cell before lock-up Interlock failure allows undetected entry
4	Water treatment system failure Make-up water system failure Pool liner failure Water level detector malfunction Piping leakage Person falls into pool
5	Failure of radiation detection system (including hand-held monitor) Interlock malfunction Control malfunction
6	Source frame jammed in transit Interlock malfunction Control malfunction
7	Electromagnetic interference Radiation damage Lack of preventative maintenance Unauthorised control modification Failure of fault indicators (heat detectors etc) Loss of power
8	Operator ignores alarms Barrier doors compromised Unauthorised control modification
9	Transport container damage due to natural causes Container damage due to transport incident Intentional disassembly of package (eg plug removed)
10	Crane failure Lifting attachment failure Sling failure Container plug falls out or is removed outside pool
11	Earthquake damage causing loss of shielding Impact from large object Flood Hurricane
12	Impact by aircraft Fire or explosion caused by product in cell Fire or explosion outside plant
13	Defective shielding material New apertures added without proper checks
14	Instrument malfunction Procedures not followed

Table 2 Failure modes leading to radioactive contamination (event numbers refer to Figure 8)

Event	*Possible failure mode*
1	Transport container contaminated at loading Undetected damaged contents Source damaged at installation in plant Loss of control of container during handling
2	Container contaminated by foreign radioactive material in transit. Other radioactive material present in area and uncontrolled
3	Weld failure - releasing contamination Capsule body failure
4	Weld failure or capsule body failure due to: (a) water not treated (b) unauthorised chemical added to water
5	Improper weld Defective capsule material
6	Product carrier impacts on source Conveyor system impacts on source
7	Source hoist mechanism interferes with source frame - out of control due to mechanical malfunction
8	Extreme damage to container due to natural hazard or collision, improper securing of container, intentional damage to container, terrorism or war
9	Loss of control of container during handling Damage to source during installation
10	Undetected source damage Undetected container contamination As result of destruction of cell by violent action
11	Due to contamination inside container cavity at initial loading
12	Due to leaking source - in water treatment area via pipework from contaminated pool
13	Contamination transferred to people from any of the previous causes

REFERENCES

1 *Ionising Radiations Regulations 1985* SI 1333/1985 HMSO ISBN 0 11 057333 1, and the IRR 1985 Approved Code of Practice COP23 HSE Books 1988 ISBN 0 11 883978 0

2 *The protection of persons against ionising radiation arising from any work activity* L58 HSE Books 1994 ISBN 0 7176 0508 6, and *Dose limitation – restriction of exposure: additional guidance on regulation 6 of the Ionising Radiations Regulations 1985 Approved Code of Practice Part 4* L7 HSE 1991 ISBN 0 11 885605 7

3 *Radiation safety for operators of gamma irradiation plants* UK Panel on Gamma and Electron Irradiation and HSE 1989

4 *Radiation safety of gamma and electron irradiation facilities* (Safety Series No 107) International Atomic Energy Agency Vienna 1992 ISBN 92 0 101692 1

5 *Health and Safety at Work etc Act 1974* chapter 37 HMSO ISBN 0 10 543774 3

6 *Food (Control of Irradiation) Regulations 1990* SI 1990/2490 HMSO ISBN 0 11 005687 6

7 *Radioactive Substances Act* 1993 chapter 12 HMSO ISBN 0 1054 1293 7

8 *Regulations for the safe transport of radioactive material ST-1* International Atomic Energy Agency Vienna 1996

9 *Radioactive Material (Road Transport) (Great Britain) Regulations 1996* SI 1996/1350 HMSO 1996 ISBN 0 11 05472 X

10 *The carriage of dangerous goods explained: Guidance for operators, drivers and others involved in the carriage of dangerous goods* Part 4 HSG162 HSE Books 1996 ISBN 0 7176 1251 1

11 *Specification for sealed radioactive sources* (*Appendix D – leak testing methods*) BS 5288: 1976

12 *The examination and testing of portable radiation instruments for external radiations* HSG49 HSE Books 1990 ISBN 0 11 885507 7

13 *Management of Health and Safety at Work Regulations 1992 Approved Code of Practice* L21 HSE Books 1992 ISBN 0 7176 0412 8

14 *Safety representatives and safety committees (The Brown Book) 3rd edition Approved Code of Practice and Guidance on the Regulations* L87 HSE Books 1996 ISBN 0 7176 1220 1

15 *A guide to the Health and Safety (Consultation with Employees) Regulations 1996* L95 HSE Books 1996 ISBN 0 7176 1234 1

16 *Safety of machinery – interlocking devices associated with guards - principles for design and selection* BS EN 1088:1996

17 *Programmable electronic systems in safety-related applications: an introductory guide* HSE Books 1987 ISBN 0 7176 1278 3, and *PES general technical guidelines* HSE Books 1987 ISBN 0 7176 0545 0. **NB This will be augmented with IEC 61508**

18 International Electrical Committee (IEC) 61508:forthcoming *Functional safety of electrical/electronic programmable safety-related systems*

19 *Safety of machinery – electrical equipment of machines Part 1 General requirements* BS EN 60204-1:1993

20 *Management of Health and Safety at Work Regulations 1992 Approved Code of Practice* L21 HSE Books 1992 ISBN 0 7176 0412 8

21 *Provision and Use of Work Equipment Regulations 1992 Guidance on the Regulations* L22 HSE Books 1992 ISBN 0 7176 0414 4

22 *Safe use of wire rope slings for general lifting purposes* BS 6210: 1983

23 *Code of Practice for the safe use of cranes* BS 5744: 1979 (partially replaced by BS 7121: Part 1: 1989 & Part 2: 1991)

24 *Code of Practice for stationary air compressors* BS 6244: 1982

25 *Specification for fusion welded steel air receivers* BS 5169: 1992

26 *Control of Substances Hazardous to Health Regulations 1994 General COSHH Approved Code of Practice* HSE Books 1997 ISBN 0 7176 1308 9

27 *Radiation protection design guidelines for 0.1-100 MeV particle accelerator facilities* National Council on Radiation Protection and Measurement, Washington (NCRP Report No 51) 1977 ISBN 0 91 339233 2

28 *The Electricity at Work Regulations* 1989 SI 1989/635 HMSO ISBN 0 11 096635 X

29 *Memorandum of Guidance on the Electricity at Work Regulations 1989* HSR25 HSE Books 1989 ISBN 0 11 883963 2

30 *Probabilistic safety assessment for large industrial irradiators* International Atomic Energy Agency Vienna 1990 IAEA-CS-93H 601

Additional reading

Henderson J and Davidson GI *Safety and the year 2000* Research Report HSE Books 1998 ISBN 0 7176 1491 3

The future availability of the publications listed in this guidance cannot be guaranteed.

Printed and published by the Health and Safety Executive
C20 10/98